Black Series

Black Series

POEMS BY

Laurie Sheck

Alfred A. Knopf
New York
2001

www.aaknopf.com

Knopf, Borzoi Books and the colophon are
registered trademarks of Random House, Inc.

Grateful acknowledgment is made to the editors of the following
publications, in which many of these poems first appeared: *The
Black Warrior Review, Boston Review, Columbia Magazine, Denver
Quarterly, The Iowa Review, The Kenyon Review,* the *New York
Times, Ontario Review, Ploughshares, Princeton University Library
Chronicle* and *The Seneca Review.*
"From Black Series: Then a Dusk Like This" appeared in *The Best
American Poetry 2000,* edited by Rita Dove and David Lehman.
"At Niaux" was included in *The Pushcart Prize: Best of the Small
Presses, 2000.*

Library of Congress Cataloging-in-Publication Data
Sheck, Laurie.
Black series : poems / by Laurie Sheck.
p. cm.
ISBN 0-375-41279-4 — ISBN 0-375-70965-7 (pbk.)
I. Title.
PS3569.H3917 B57 2001
811'.54—dc21
                  2001029928

Manufactured in the United States of America
First Edition

Thanks to the National Endowment for the Arts, for a
Literature Fellowship awarded during the writing of this book.

My deepest gratitude to David Mayer.

To Jim and Maia

Contents

I / Black Series

The Store Windows Glitter

Even the mannequins change
as the headlights pass over them, swathing them
in strangeness. A face briefly lit, magnetized by
street light. Or an arm vibrating, as if to touch the shocked
surfaces, cracked sidewalks and neon-scald of walls,
while the other arm, unlit, sleeps on, apart from the whirring
interventions, shut doorways stung by light,
zig-zagging shadows, grown animate with each anxious
and precise erasure, advancing like hostile take-overs
onto the newly minted glass.
I feel the unstable atoms in my skin, nerve-paths roughened
by the smallest detonations.

There's quietness a moment, then the mannequins
are lit again, and wake, each face a sentry's raw, uncluttered mind
buffeted by night-sounds, currents thickening and knotting in the leafy
air, where listening is a kiss slowly changing in another's
open mouth.

If there be abundant sand left (there is not)
If there be certainty and stillness (there is not)
If there be stalled brilliances and volatile undoings
If there be fraught silence
trackless night—

Look how the store windows glitter. Irradiated
mirrors, strenuous slashings over the false alarms
of the mannequins' smooth faces. The mannequins standing
too whitely, as in illness. And above them,

through the smog, the moon's light's a gauzy dress, pierced
and tattered, twirling gravely downward, heavy with its own undoing,
falling in a slow relentless drowning.

Then there's quietness again. Then flashing sirens—
the mannequins putting on color as red lights twist past their windows
giving them red wings, red wings growing out of each shoulder, rippling

and lifting

over the envious
silver, prisoned glass.

Then a Dusk Like This

Then a dusk like this, a subversion of surfaces,
a vague expectancy of absence. Blurrings. Wings.
I watch the edges break and flee; they are Ophelias.

Soft town that settles on this land, town of inconclusiveness,
encryption, I touch your gateless air, your scaffoldless
upholdings. What covenants do you carry as you come,
what summonings provisioning your kingdom, and all the footless
crossings that move through you? What treaties and what pacts?
Blown leaves against the rotting fence, the jutting tilted heads
of rusted nails, they drift in a suspended radiance
that floods the skin like fear but isn't fear.

The yellow mullein stand tall against the house
as though they know they must negotiate this passage
as you conjure them away, your brain-darks reeling,
your glimmerings revising, interceding,
yet somehow they return by morning.

Now the sun's transit has gone under. The smallest splinterings
asleep it seems. Asleep the clear-lit custody of knowing.
Soft town, I am your citizen, though I'm knot and barb
among your wanderings, and can feel the fraught circuitries
first calm then slash themselves in me, resisting,
the wanting-to-be-calmed extending itself to you
then pulling fiercely back, self-maiming,
and this grazing of fingertips like wind, these nervous fingertips
like wind —

doubt is a beautiful garment, if only I could wear it,
all silk and ashes, on my skin.

Meanwhile the Lilies Start to Close

Meanwhile the lilies start to close
as if withdrawing from the fragility of the outer meanings.
Green-house bred, delicate,
each looks like an x-rayed hand, fingers clenched and bending,
flaring whitely where the rays Roentgen discovered by mistake
and named X for the unknown
have entered them in every dimension.

My window holds a row of billboards.
Borderland of faces, of mouths and mouths and mouths
like flawed computations, and eyes always open, over the echoing
prosperity, each face an admission ticket to something the wind
doesn't move through, can't blow down.

A man out walking his dog passes underneath the billboards.
If I could hear his heartbeat . . .
his face not digitalized, the swervings that must be in him,
the secret swayings and severest
wonderment, amazement, under this most vivid distrust,
most vivid caution. . . .

I hear him calling to the dog,
Let's go now boy, it's time now boy, let's go.
So small they look, like toys beneath the billboards.
Softness of skin, of hesitance, kingdom of invisible echoes and delays,
raw flesh of lilies, and fog over the city now,
and antimatter, particles, black holes, erased lullabies, forgotten wing—

in this *meantime* I watch the man walk home
through threshold after threshold of his thoughts opening and unfolding,
admitting and releasing him, grazing his skin
and searing him or calming him, and how I cannot feel them, cannot know.

So Fast Away

Think hands, think mouth, think eyes. Those pieces floating
in their stream of thought. That they might cohere and be a life,
life lived, in one room or another, footfall and laughter,
signs over doorways, moving air. That the mouth might speak,

the eyes watch, the ears listen. Listen to each paraphrase,
see the wind-threaded passagings, the errors like pathways
leading to a door, what door? That the tongue remember the taste
of salt, the ears the sweep of wind and rain, mice clawing

at the walls. Everything's blowing away so fast.
So fast away. Myself away. Think hands, think mouth, think eyes,
how silent the unbecoming is, how silent the unraveling. So much
of thinking happens in the light's receding, the fade-out into black,

the I was there and then I wasn't there—I remember
that spire, that roof, that bell—and now I'm here.
As if for a reason. Fade to black. Fade slowly now to black.
And the mouth says at night, when no one hears,

I loved the blown pages, the torn ones, they were the only ones
I loved. The scatterings in them, the silences still seeding
them, the gaps and rottings, terrain of disappearances,
of presences half-caught and fleeing, words ripped

as if lightning had scorched them, claimed them for its own.
These hands and eyes. Soft mouth that spoke and couldn't speak.

Hands that touched and didn't touch. Eyes that hungered and withstood,
all over the sensitized surfaces, the surfaces of things keenly layered,

undeluded. The love of structure and the love of wind. At night thinking
                                                                    scatterings
and eyes. Thinking lightning and surfaces and fade. It's black, it is so dark
though traceries of light are still adrift in this somewhere, scatter-shot and hidden.
When no one can hear. When touched. When scattered. When hidden. When
                                                                    watched.

Driving Home

Here in this decentered light, this sizzling, reeling hum,
I remember the moon's face, its calm remove, or so it seemed,
its white volition. Here there are "selling points,"
here, as the car radio tells me, there are "stopgap measures"
to be taken, and tradings and loans.

Once the night was medicinal. Doctorly, it leaned.
I felt its starched coat against my cheek, its stethoscope
measuring. The heartbeats came steadily, trusting
what would meet them; I sensed their quiet
venturing, each hushed and embryonic expedition.
They weren't like weapons inspectors
alert to subterfuge, sniffing out concealment.
Wariness stood to the side, only watching;
she seemed undesirous of speech, peering
through the night's lullaby walls, much like a pauper.

This night sky's a delirium pulsing
with buzzing neon signs, and the dizzying auras they breed.
The faces beneath them pass in strangeness, they go and come
and pause in leery strangeness, hybrids of neon and flesh,
the light filtering into their hair, gliding under
their skin, sipping at their eyes, their lips.
It is so thirsty, the neon, leaning down onto my windshield,
where my face can neither give consent
nor recoil and disallow its touch.

Sound-bites labor through the air, configuring
then fading, passing through this line of cars,
rising into somewhere we can't see.
All the pastures of clicking channels drifting in the netted dark;
in one a bidding war, in one the newest gadget,
latest craze. And netted, too, the small voice of self
saying I am tangled and encoded, saying I am wave-toss, I am riddle,
bridled wind. The self that is like lightning flaring through a lullaby,
while Venus glides above us, and above us, too, all the unimaginable planets,
their blameless light so far from here, so wordless, unconstrained.

The Mannequins

How can they know uncertainty, the mannequins,
as they stand behind their glass, austere
as apothecary jars lined up on dusted shelves,
the radium-glow of the window distilling their whitenesses,
faintest residue of fingerprints crumbled and releasing?
The night air is mossy on my skin, a soft confusing mouth,
but they have been propped in their poses where gesture is already elegy,
stiff in the elemental light of their withdrawal. The window is a cargo boat,
an edict authorizing a cold reflected stillness.

Outside their world is the fragility of movement,
metonymic displacements, as leaves of the black poplar
mix with the music from high buildings
that filters down, torn and partial, out of its first tenderness.
Footsteps, sirens, slamming doors, tattoo
this frameless night I walk through, its harsh economy of rumor and of wind.

Backlit and leaning toward the street, the mannequins
look almost curious, as if wondering how it feels to be complicit
with the ebb and flow of light, how a face
can't discern itself; its territories shift and are shadowed,
a shore that wavers, its conduct ever conscripting,
raw and soft with trespass.

If a voice never stuttered, if the air were smooth and smooth only,
how horrible the surfaces would be then, shiny lures
pinned to a board, never touching water.
Heel-clicks. Leaf-fall. Jangling keys.

I feel the cracked asphalt under my shoes, all the breakages
kindled and released by motion. This night filled with edges
and with shifts. My skin inside it, my skin its creature,
while the smooth unstartled mannequins stand whitely in their windows
that shine like computer screens, incarnate and withheld.

In Curious May

I didn't want to only dream in black and white,
but when the colors came back
they frightened me, the reds I'd thought I craved, their technicolor
poisons shimmering, an errant lens, a gauzy burning
dress.

Smooth forms deceive,
give way to their own chaos. It seemed all equal signs
had fallen off the earth—
or was the earth singing equivalences
I couldn't catch?
I could feel the breaking webs, each vexed and battered
hesitance like wind, the crucial wreckage
of the cover stories flaring and dissolving like burnt footage,
daylilies opening, as in a dream of staying.
What is steady? What is not usurped?

In curious May I felt my mind become a place where filthy wings
of screech owls break apart, where dead twigs blossom
in the mud, where roots and stems are culled from riverbanks
to harm and sometimes heal, where bewildered trees awaken
and can't move, where slit necks drink in potions that renew
them, and questions prowl stream-like through the dirt
only to end at moss-covered rocks
that never answer.

I could feel the intertwinings as they moved in and out of me,
hurrying over my open eyes, my skin, as if I was watching
many films at once, and they were entering each other

as I watched, their colors swirling, blending in,
horizon lines collapsing,
voices breaking beneath the weight of many voices.

Once I lay in a white room, as if I wasn't born.
A plain unmutilated place beside the sea.
In the next room a couple held and kissed each other,
yellow loosestrife bright outside the window, then the stars.

Bridal Veil

On the crest of the far hill, the lone tree
with bare black branches is Medusa's head,
her snake-hair spitting stars into the sky.
I would hack her at the neck,
watch color and movement flood back into the world.
The eyes in her hair, like the intricate, stopped workings
of a clock, would press against the ground,
and the tongues harden, roads to nowhere, blue in the blue light.

Then reds and oranges will startle back, awake,
hawkweed spreading through the fields
like the hurt, violent silence after requiem.
The children will braid wildflowers
into the horses' manes and tails.
Dull green as dollar bills, the tall grasses barely waver,
but when wind and noonlight flood them
their silvery undersides rise up to cut the stillness.
Their shivering doesn't frighten me;
it is not a nervous thing. It knows nothing of the fever fed by fear.

Far from the rigidity of mannequins
the lambs wander over the back fields.
Thistles stick to their foreheads, such ragged, misplaced crowns.
Across the road, two horses rub against the fence,
flies feeding at their eyes.
A car gleams in its metallic estrangement,
odd creature with shiny purple skin.

This is the kingdom that quickens and won't sleep;
the fierce ignited light of tenderness, unburied.
Tonight the moon will rise
full and white, like Medusa's murdered face.
But she will turn nothing to stone. I have my hawkweed in a bowl,
orange-red as Chinese silk, a fiery bridal veil, a vow.
It is this my eyes will close on.

Medusa

I can almost taste the glassy air. Where are the birds in it,
wings lifting as currents buffet them like echoes, bright
chaos of atomized instances,
storm-light gashing, hurrying, dispersing? I can almost taste
the stillness. Are there faces in front of me? Are there eyes?
And tongues in a gathering wilderness of mouths? Always it is strange
to watch them change when he lifts me from the sack and makes me look—

my eyes a chisel, then a shroud, wrapping them,
colorless, frozen there, all stone.
Inside the sack I remember the soft
contorted flickerings of skin
before I drew my gaze completely up
and entered, still amazed at how my eyes
enact their mandate. And I think of how, from out of my own body

(which is lost to me now, rotting in some nameless place,
torso, arms and legs gone piece-meal, mossy, rank) a horse with wings
was born, flying up past dirt, past swirling
dust, into the winds that sweep past stone,
past all the dead and trees and leaning stems, and past the steady
weapons of my eyes. How did that horse come to grow
in me, that winged and unbound thing? It was like
something I dreamt, a whispering I might have heard

in the long-ago of light and mist and rain
imprinting unreadable coins on the rooftops.
What is safety? How can the world shelter itself
from itself? If I could stay blindfolded forever—

and not turn each thing into a caption, rigid and shatterless,
perfectly intact. There are quick particles of light
behind my eyes, neurons acidly scattering
small suns, unhooded sky (or my body, wholly lost to me now, or the horse's
wings prospering and beating). Then I taste the glassy air again,
hear the steady breathing, and then the hands (I think of them
as voices speaking on a soundtrack that re-winds,
repeats, repeats) reaching to undo
the sack, lift me into sunlight, make me look.

Instructions for a Black and White Photograph

1.   Keep distance in.

2.   Angle a white cloth in the foreground of the interior front door.

3.   The door open. The floor broad wooden planks.

4.   Long view of the back window, its brittle whiteness holding one bare tree, a form of grace or hiding.

5.   Who lives here?

6.   What place is not an oblique place?

7.   So many crooked footsteps leading to the doorway, invisible presences, sealed envelopes, dissolving words.

8.   Molecules colliding, creating a steady pressure on the walls.

9.   Mute angle of light across the floor (So like a sleeping body).

10.   What will chance bring? What will the shadows bring?

11.   The white cloth bunched and crumpled, a desolate or joyful love, a body remembering something it can't speak, no mouth to it, its cadences phantomed and gathered away—

12.   Keep distance in. Keep silence.

13.   Who lives here?

14.   (The shadows are articulate although they will not speak.)

Circuits

Again the dark begins to meddle with the buildings,
first softening then releasing them
that they might fold themselves back into concealment,
while the silences wander, inexhaustible, diverse,
hovering like shame and not like shame,
dispersing over neon-shattered streets.

But the programmed air is purposeful and sure; it doesn't wander.
It carries a deliberateness inside it,
a brittleness like wooden boxes.
In my neighbor's room, electronic voices soothe him,
and bodies made of an uncertain light
that pass back and forth through brief episodic disclosures.
No microbes live in them, or stenches—only a blue glow.
Each night they become their own erasures.

The circuits that guide me are smaller than I know.
What gaunt liberty this is, this waiting for headlines,
the flesh drenched in hearsay,
or the distant, lovely algebra of stars,
the offer that is good for one week only.
Outside, the raw data of the faces pass.
Someone is tearing a photograph in thirds. Someone
is laughing. Someone is stockpiling rage,
sharp words about to burst into the throat.
Where is the soundtrack? Where the poison dress to sting me clean?
How quiet chaos is. How tracelessly it enters.

The Flowers

As if no harm will stir in the flawed radiance

of the horizon line   grown rich with interruptions

rooftops   phone wires   branch upon branch poking, intertwining

and the mouths of flowers opening against skin   their vivid

unprotected softness   (precarious, enduring wish)

               as if no harm would even stir

while the mind's making catalogues of flowers:

               loosestrife, poppy, thistle, hawkweed, rose,

and the many-stemmed daylilies   each blossom like a day's headlines
                                      burgeoning

then left behind, while the new one offers itself

               in untranslated peacefulness

outside of the contingencies   of touch   and of this skin

which in itself is fragile, discontinuous   anxiety entranced with expectation

among the zig-zagging paths of pollen grains   and the symmetries, asymmetries

and the tongues of conscience   and the tongues of coveting and wonder and *feather of lead, cold fire, bright smoke, still-waking sleep,*

                         the mind remembering

the race of the midstream, the momentary acts, the strange perpetual weaving

                                   and unweaving. . . .

As if no harm will stir in me,

                        in this harsh interior dark I can't decipher,

or in one thing eclipsed or altered by another,

or in the names spray painted dayglo green

                lingering even now in tender unconcealed abundance

as when selenite grows ever whiter with the waxing moon.

How calming the encumbrances are   how like a love that must be overthrown,

a stubborn instance held to from without—

                the slow burn of the horizon line

and the flowers beneath it   thriving and efficient in their way.

The Cave

I woke in the black night and thought,
"It's the black night that wakes in me," its pupils merciless, unseeing.
The window camouflaged as if by my own ignorance.
No moon. If it were daylight the mountains would still be lost in fog.
All day my eyes couldn't petition them back.

It's the black night that wakes in me, so dominant, so focused.
And then a car goes by and I think, "I'm in the world,"
tires kicking up gravel from the dust.
What does the orange hawkweed do inside this dark—its radiance
secretive but not extinguished?

Radio static flicks at the air, all the stillnesses crackling,
edged pathways of some neural damage. And then the voices are unwound
from their static-shroud—I hear them—talking, talking,
and music's twisting through them
until the static rounds them up and gathers them back in. . . .

Once I walked inside a cave wide and high-domed past its narrow
entrance. There was a battery-operated torch to carry. Pictures
stared from the gray walls. Stags. And buffaloes. And horses.
One with eyes closed. And many with their backs washed off
from centuries of damp, some with arrows hanging from their sides,
others with their young worn down to nothing more than tiny graceful hooves.
There in the closed laughing dark where they lived, and our trespass.
That laughing dark held them, was their home, the place of their belonging.

I woke in the black night and thought: petitioner of distance, pauper,
bankrupt owner of some torn-up deed, my eyes are Cinderella
untransformed, her gray dress spread round her ankles, her feet cool and bare
in the cool ash that rings the fireplace (no matter how much she sorts she won't
complete the task, not ever) while mice dart back and forth out of the walls,

laden, like her, with the fierce gift of such ignorance, such hunger.

Foal

The lesion-stars whiten
    over the hidden blooms and wind-bent grasses
while herded up from the ground, extravagant, fireflies
    inscribe against the trees a green circuitry, acid,
edged as trauma.
    The mountain behind them unseized, untamed by mutilation.
No hunger inside it. Only itself and itself.

No Town gathers me in. Computer hum in the air, faint
    whirring, soft clacking of keys
as if padded. Whose fingers do I hear?
    But no Town gathers me, no *in*.

The field of unknowing opens where the foal
    went running. It was brown with white spots,
its right rear foot torn where the barbed wire snagged it
    in the lightning-gash of storm. I ran my fingers
through its mane. It bent its neck, hesitant, deliberate,
    a precise consideration.

A restlessness, a broken fence: are they
    a Town? Are they the Town that calls?
Town of damage and desire, of the brown neck bending
    toward the grass, and the ignorant hands, the fumbling
uncertain hands, stroking, pausing—lost in the trespass,
    learning the unstillness—stroking.

The Horses

So quiet now, the wind a most delicate hurt
gone into hiding. If I could touch its untraceable
wanderings, its cascades unsettling the grasses,
if I could hear its rough lullaby that has
no need to ask *but with what wings? what poisons*
burning, seeping, or what fire? then I could feel
the thrall of pathlessness, its scrawls not tamed
by false conclusions, under the volatile blurrings of the stars.

The sea raises its black horse-heads, shining necks.
I bend to listen, as I've listened to the air
kissing into me, carrying reports of serial-killers,
and listened to it rushing over newly minted bills,
and over storefronts covered with graffiti,
flower-stalls where lilies stand in plastic buckets.

Broadcast-light flickers, torn and adamant, against the wall.
It would slash the sea's black horses,
or eat away at them like acids.
But the horses lift their heads out past the rocks,
their eyes unbewildered by
this livid inside light.

The dark gathers nothing. It's not acquisitive,
merely agile. A gentle covering, or harsh, depending.
I feel it unwrap itself as if it weren't monitored,
the datascapes and pixels foraging somewhere else, collecting,
while the horses run through pastures I can't see,
black radiance of hoofbeats, black fetlocks, streaming manes.

Memory Palaces

1

But I wanted the colors back. The astounding openness in them. Wanted what Cicero desired for his memory palaces: "we set up images and assign to them exceptional beauty or singular ugliness . . . we dress some with crowns or purple cloaks, or we disfigure them, as by introducing stained blood or mud or red paint." And in this way we will remember them.

2

You are carrying red zinnias. The sky's pale yellow. That taxi is yellow and black, its window-frame silver. Those leaves are orange, indifferent to distrust. No, those leaves are pale green. Distrust is purple, or it is very white, like arsenic or raw silk. Speed is blue then gold; it will wear nothing. That commentary is covered in wet blood. That hand is gloved. What color is the glove? What color is the hand? Blue is patient, it knows how to hide, it knows what waiting is. The rain is blue and also the river and the sun.

3

A memory palace seems too grand. Maybe I'll just take that turn of road, brown and unprotected. I'll leave a woolen hat. A fork, a spoon, a knife. A bottle of water and of wine. My shame is a red fog; it settles on the road. There's the gold scrap of someone's laughter. Hand tracing my spine in the night.

4

Once, while attending a gathering at the palace, Simonides stepped outside for air, and a split-second later the whole ceiling collapsed. Everyone inside was killed. But because he valued order and remembering, he could recall the exact placement and seating arrangements of the guests. The crushed, unrecognizable bodies were handed over to the proper relatives for burial and mourning, while Simonides pointed, calling out each name.

5

This window-frame is silver. Kindness is many colors, impossible to name. A storm changes my section of brown road. Red dust, green dust. The rain is blue and also the river and the sun.

Pompeii

Covered with lapilli we crouch preserved as we were on that first day

The last one of our lives

Our bodies black marginalia beneath the sky's unstable searchlight

They have unearthed the House of the Fawn the House of the Silver Wedding

And the Surgeon's House

Our bread still in our ovens

Our tables spread and set

They have unearthed our lamp factories our fulleries the things

We wrote on walls

They lift our rigidity up into

Sunlight we no longer see

Our eyes night sky

And because we cannot speak

It seems to them we're holding many secrets

The Burned Tree

No comment, the TV-mouth said, the buzzing
caught inside the screen like caged, elliptic wings,
the mouth feeding its few words into the microphone's soft waiting,
into the tape recorder's gray imprinted cave.
And then a voice said *stay tuned to this same station,*
but there are so many crossings the mind desires; I wanted to set out,
to feel the sweet pulsations of being; I wasn't caught in black and white,
not part of that, not tethered to a screen.

I looked out onto the meadow.
The burned tree hadn't completely disappeared,
though its trunk, so large and solid months ago, was gone.
Coils of tumbled branches
lay entangled with a network of stray roots
whorled and meshed against the hill,
and inside their intertwinings, hiding places formed,
intervals, encampments,
the tree uttering its quenchless thirst into the air,
its swarming northwinds and southwinds unforgotten,
the unwritten history of its swayings, its furious amplitude
still coveted and breathing through those branches.

Only last fall it had been standing.
I loved the measureless gardens of its winds,
its unconstellated thrashings,
such transcriptless possibilities, flickerings, becomings. . . .

So still its trunk, back then, and yet the leaves
couldn't help but journey,

the man-made frequencies riding high above them,
not touching them at all,
whereas they entered me with such delicate unerring ease,
my head full of jingles, of the car radio's static, of the weather forecast
I'd heard while driving down North Hill.

And now this tree, what's left of it,
heaped in this night's increasing dark, and enmeshed
with plastic bottles, beer caps, shattered glass,
seems to me so much like a face the dark is taking back
into its sweetnesses, its secret annexations
—as if in kindness, almost as in kindness—

away from my cautious eyes, my word-bound eyes.

No Printout

Sundown, and the hills grow vague
as if giving a secret kindness to themselves
now that our human eyes can't scrutinize their properties
or pillage them for solace.
And it seems I am dissolving as I watch,
I who am nothing more than nothing now . . .
as the hard and cunning edges break apart, the sharp
currency of day eroding, finally governed by such softness,
my beggar-eyes scanning, looking for a channel that's not there.

I feel the turns and counter-turns of air,
a rustling as of cloth, voice-scrap, rave of wind.
There's the flick of a lit match, fitful webbings of headlights
up the road. A voice saying *Buy one get one free.*
Light pulses on and off in nearby windows
the way a meandering grief pauses at one place and then another
as if to sip from them awhile before it pushes further on,
no printout disfiguring its leaving.

Branches multiply in air, gather past the window.
In this, my printless feet, my eyes unambushed and unambushing,
my hands. . . . Hills, the layered darks now take you.
Or have you become the dark that enwraps you, as once a girl
became a tree, her leaves swaying in that freedom,
her sudden facelessness her joy.

II / The Crossing

Sun

Reared in the cave of the wild north wind, my Father . . .

and then how the sun felt on my skin that first time, almost vicious—

its scorched vigilance prospered on the smallest things:

a button, a fly, a wren, a pair of lips.

Each thing wrenched from its own darkness, gleaming.

~~~

So the sun touched me and I felt its ownership of me.

I watch the birds like a white sea, the doors, the wheels, the window-boxes, rocks.
I watch the poppies flare and wither,
cloud-surge over hills, migratory shadows over faces and on fields;
veil of, code of—

I watch the pond the malady of stillness.
I watch the yoke upon the horse's neck, I watch its reins, its saddle, blindered eyes.

Steel, tin, strangers, dust.
The crevices in rocks like fallen arrows. I watch the day-moon and the stars.
The whole business of profit and loss.

~~~

Could have hidden could have railed could have sickened could have wandered
could have prowled could have stolen could have spoken could have hungered
could have planted could have whispered could have stumbled could have sung

~~~

When the sun rises it casts dull blades across the fields,
and later fanatical sharpnesses, contours edged like mania,
roofs, waves, tables, walls, tracked down like thieves
and gripped within that fierce exposure.

Then slowly the softening creeps in, kissing and lingering,
or it's as if an eye has grown quite tired,
wanting only the filmy cloth of veil, wanting only the blurred, dispersing world.

~~~

The cave's far off now, who knows where. Ever smaller
in my mind, thin as a dropped stick of gum.
No headlines lived in it, no cover stories, times or dates.
The sea sounding always like the sea. I couldn't change the channel.

There are so many construction sites here, so many scaffoldings and trenches.
Neon flashes on and off as if cutting itself, marring further the nervous
thinness of its skin. Gray screens carry their simulcasts

while light wanders through them, a moor made of water, liquid hills.
There are intentions, questions, lies. Yellow petals and then red.

The air is full of thresholds and nets.
Sparrows break from the phone wires, scatter off into a blue-white sky.

Wall-Writing

The busyness of these walls. The scrawls on them,
    the names and peeling posters. DOREEN. TRAGIC MAGIC. ARE YOU THERE?
I'm walking where the city splits from its glossy
    exteriors and the streets veer off, cramped and narrow,

refusing to be anonymous, clean.
    Where the world builds in them—angers, anarchies
of scarring, tears. Spray-painted. Glaring and worn.
    All these bright colors as if trying to cover
a secret, quiet pain, or to make that pain rise through them,
    wrapping it in shining swirls and markings,

until it shimmers, less fretful, less alone.
    Lifting it, almost tenderly—
infant-soft, fragile—
    up into the world. . . .
I pass the store windows, mannequins and flashy glass,

my face moving over them, over the line-up of eyes, the limbs,
    the usual suspects, broken tribes.
So that I am momentarily one of them, frozen, caged,
    my face wedged in
above the price tags hanging from their wrists.

There's the cut of a siren, then the cut of screeching tires.
    But I want to stay still a moment, want to watch how these walls
have blossomed
    with graffiti, how the blanknesses surrendered, the wildness
and stern unyielding wanting

transforming them into all color and givenness
    unguarded. Unguarded! Here in this landscape that's not
forgetfulness and not defeat. This landscape that's not the
    annihilation of pain, though it's pain and annihilation—and then

what comes from pain, what answers pain.

Broken Window

What inside me will finance the trespass, the unprisoning?
Outside there's neon seeping into brick, destabilizing each wall-face,
my eyes a faint hesitance over it, two shadows merely passing.
Taxi-lights circle the block, muffled as aftershock,
and everything's "in transit" — but to where?

I've been like the iced black glare of a window,
too still. That glare so paralyzed, severe.
I've felt the web-sites untouchable and safe above me,
sites of data-banks and pixels, sites that *repeal the beating ground,*
until softness seemed a perilous intent, and myself a mere artifact
from a waywardness long over. And the things I'd thought of as my life —

had they happened after all, or had I seen them on some screen?
In black and white or color?
As if each moment had grown hooded, tranced,
consoled and buffered by the vaguest distance.
In the dream when the iced black window broke I saw what was behind
it: scorched earth and the match in my hand. The farthest fields

still burning. Searchlights over the brown hills.
So this is what I've disavowed, I thought, and it's come back finally
to find me. The face (my face) turned away when it realized
I watched it, not wanting to be seen. There was no broadcast

to distract me, no quick commercial break. Rapture
is seeing. The fields glowed with the stark abandon of ruin,
miles of ash traversed by many footprints.
I must walk into this, I thought, carrying my tarnished wishes,
so many texts and road maps water-marked and damaged,
my hands opening without forethought or conclusion or the false unmoving

safety of a frame.

Traces

The gaze needs to be healed, I thought. I felt the fretful networks in my eyes
seeded by light, longing toward the light-struck grass,
and also toward the stars, felt the eye's legacy of scavenging,
desire. What laws guide our seeing?
Here, unscripted, how do we see?

Stalks of yellow loosestrife stand tall against the glassed-in porch,
and above them, kept from sight because it's day, the stars'
barely-linked configurations, terrain where emptiness and pulsings
meet; this vast field I live in but can't know and hardly see.

~~~

Aerial Photograph of Weapons Disposal Site, Toole Army Depot, Toole, Utah

How do I belong to this? Landscape of process, of memory traces,
    of light animating disfigurement, disfigurement animating light,
landscape that almost everything in me
        wants to push away.

Where has the eye's hunger gone to now?

And then suddenly I want to look—the glowing skin of earth
    solemnly enchanted, its ruined silver-darks
ridged with memory traces still cleaving to each surface, the intricate designs of
                                                                                    process
        seeming to enter the ear as well as eye,
until they are a chorus, hooded, singing.

It looks like the cratered moon,
    but with scratches on it, long gouges, pin-like, from Jocasta's brooch.
Oedipus's eyes in the riveted baseline of aftermath. The scratches glow
    and are beautiful, as if longing, strong and always, toward the light.
More helter-skelter than an ancient script, but still a writing, ruinous and
                                                     starkly pure.

    As if not made by human thought.

~~~

"I asked the earth, and it answered me, 'I am not He,' and whatsoever are in it confessed the same. I asked the sea, and the deeps, and the living creeping things, and they answered, 'We are not thy God, seek above us.' I asked the moving air; and the whole air with its inhabitants answered, 'Anaximenes was deceived, I am not God.' I asked the heavens, sun, moon, stars, 'Nor say they are we the God whom thou seekest.' And I replied unto all the things which encompass the door of my flesh, 'Ye have told me of my God, that ye are not He; tell me something of Him.' And they cried out with a loud voice, 'He made us.' My questioning them was my thoughts on them: and their form of beauty gave the answer."

~~~

Aerial Photograph of Sedan Crater, Nevada Test Site

When vaporized earth collapses
    at an underground detonation site

this is what is left: a gaping crater in the shape of a wide
    and laughing mouth. The sun on the horizon's
reflected in the crater as it sets, so that it seems there are two suns at once,
    one for the earth's unbroken surface, and one to travel farther downward
through the mouth. Sky-glow, calm as harbor, word-emptied, resplendent,
    darkens slightly at the edges, and I imagine, in the distance, a fire
walking toward it.

~~~

Abeyance of stars, blacknesses of night, the undisfigured place
between each footfall;
my flashlight marks, as I walk, the smallest portionings of field, untended.
Grasses, hidden nests. . . .

The gaze wants to be healed, I thought. But now the darkness sings to it,
lullaby of wanderings and hiddenness, cricket-noise, brief wind.
Feel the soft grasses, it says, you don't have to look,
just feel them under your sneakers, don't worry about being healed, only feel
                                                            this—
abundance of darks, of softnesses unmapped, uncaptured.

~~~

After the banquet, Cesi described the joy of Galileo and his friends as they
climbed onto the rooftop where the new instrument, the telescope, was set:
"Every serene evening we see new things in the heavens: Jupiter with his
four satellites and their distinct periods . . . the cavernous, wandering moon,

cuckolded Venus and the triple star of Saturn. . . . These observations cause no small difficulty for the old theory that the earth is the center of the universe."

And Galileo wrote of how the moon wasn't robed in a smooth, polished surface as they'd been taught, but was "uneven, rough, full of cavities and prominences not unlike the face of earth." And "It glows with an uncertain light."

~~~

The gaze wants to be healed, I thought. It is filled with an uncertain light.

There is
no other light.

But if the gaze were healed it wouldn't journey. The gaze is wounded and doesn't want to be healed.

~~~

My Dear Friend Diodati,

I write to you from my prison in Arcetri. Alas I, your friend and servant Galileo, have been for the last month hopelessly blind, so that this heaven, this earth, this universe, which I with my eyes did love, has shrunk to such a small space as is filled only by my bodily sensations.

And yet in my mind I often see them—sun spots, moon, Jupiter rising, the belt and sword of Orion, all my starry messengers; my spy glass aimed at the sky

47

that floods us with its laws, its wonders. The moon's visage looks down on us sometimes with its chin turned a little to the right, sometimes to the left, as it is the arbiter and superintendent of our oceans.

Early mornings and nights I hear the two pigeons in the dovecote, singing.

~~~

Aerial Photograph of Minuteman II Missile Silo, Pawnee National Grassland, Colorado

Why does the ground look full of swirls
    like a child's sand-drawing, or a hand's delighted motion in the waves?
And then within those swirls
    there's a rectangular enclosure — is that a wall or a self-meeting road? —
                                            within which
the missile silo stands like a small toy.
    Outside the walls, though, is desire, the earth
holding itself stalk by stalk and grain by grain
    apart from us,
the upheavals of millennia, the shifting of tectonic plates,
    inscribed and still conversing on its body.

~~~

All day the field floods like fever. Mirrory, pulsing, unstill.
As if a disorder of stars had come to nest there.
Irruptive swarms, then calmnesses, autochthonous stirrings
so different from the hemmed-in laws of streets. Not safe as in a film-clip,
ever-building. My gaze unhooks

into its stormy brightnesses, its brightnesses a song
by which the mind self-haunts and labors.

The grasses wild and dancing as they drown.

The Carpenter Bees

The carpenter bees are drilling smooth, perfect holes in the side of the house,
holes the size of bullets. I watch them at their task,
the flowers in their summery brilliances beneath them.
It is not petals they want. It is not softness.
No matter how hard I look I can't see where they lay their eggs
in the bare, unpainted wood, or how they clean and provision their nest, its
                                        many cells.
Doubt is a foreign land they've never entered.

The wood is sweet, like pollen. All afternoon they carve it
like small coffins, Egyptian boats they'll sail into the starry blackness.
They are meticulous and sure, unlike my skin which feels
the wind's shiftings and grows confused, turning toward the chill and then the
                                         heat,
my skin stitched with unknowing, so that although I stand firmly on the ground

I always feel I am drifting away. That there is nothing but to drift away.
They are the size of thimbles. If they were hollow I could slip them on my
                                         fingers;
I'd feel their workings, the texture of their mission, how they're programmed
like a missile, heading for the wood to bore their holes.
They can't know that tonight at sunset when they've burrowed

toward their queeny sleep, a man will come with a spray-can and aim it
at their home. Later he'll fill their drilled city
with wood-colored putty. In their dreamless sleep
they'll fall, one by one, out of their calm harbor. And I will miss

their steady aim, their certainty, the way they used the minutes with such
patience. The way they sculpted, carved. When the clouds pass over the fields
I watch their blurrings, as if they were hurrying to cover us with horrible gray
                                                          gauze.
As if they understood I can't withstand their drownings, the darkenings they
                                                         bring me.
The wings of the carpenter bees will disintegrate bit by bit in sunlight,
the poison rising from their bodies, their purposeless stillness hardening, dulling.
But for now they are at their work, the holes they carve like the cave

found by the girl who was half-bird, and who wanted to hide herself
in shame from human eyes; to keep the secret of her jutting beak, her wings,
while the walls dripped all about her their tinny, lilting music,
the clouds outside so quiet, more distant than the stars.

Waking

Waking, I held the disintegrating dream against my skin.
    The fresh wind of early morning entered. I watched the white curtains
pulse and breathe,
            felt their winged enchantment. A lightness lifting the room
where the pieces of dream
        still clung to me, flotsam, shards—the infant lifted from deep water still
                                                                    alive,
the paper I'd been forced to sign in a khaki-colored room
            that meant a child would be taken
into another room
            and disappear forever.

~~~

The ocean like a delicate hand
        and then, later, like a palsied hand. Unfrightened sky
above the hidden coral,
        dark hospital of eyes, some fish-eaten,
others gelatinous and cloudy, still whole.

Here is the mind's disjunctive hush—disturbance of waves
        over the terrain of ocean floor, uneven.
I heard it in my dream as I watched the infant
        lifted from the silvery
realm; I who should have kept it from harm
        was afraid to look into its eyes
then a pulse jumped
        in its neck

an unfathomable softness trembled
       and my eyes became my hands became the sea. . . .

until the dream-sea gave way to this real one
    where I walk;
its carnage mostly covered
      except of course for what's always washing up: today, part of a fish
pine-green and gleaming, pink shells
    like dollhouse dishes,
plastic bottles, tinfoil, cigarette butts, vertebrae, rusted lures.

~~~

Why would Perseus treat the severed head of Medusa with such gentleness,
    preparing with great care a bed of leaves
and sea grasses on which to set it down? Her stare, even through the sack,
    could harden the lithe seaweeds into coral, could turn the leaves
to brittle gleaming scales.

He laid her softly down,
    that weight he knew so well, weight of the terrible eyes, the hissing hair,
having carried it always since he'd slain her.
    Kept her there
while he washed his hands of blood.

Was it his shadow-self he carried?
    Was it his knowledge of the world?

The stare the head the snakes the hissing hair
      not a foreign country at all
but close as his beating heart, intimate, incarnate,

though there was also the matter of his hands, the gentleness still in them,
      the desire
              to not do harm.

~~~

Inside the burlap sack the head, I think, is dreaming.
      She feels the hands hold her with gentleness,
feels the gathered bed of leaves and seaweeds
      as she's laid down
as in a field of sun and light-tipped grasses, but it is always dark now.
      Dreaming: everything gray as if xeroxed,

but the figures move, their arms and legs
      writing themselves in cursive over sand and in the sea.
The light uninfected, unbesieged. Wavebrights frictioning.
      She is jealous of their freedom to configure,
reconfigure.

Dreaming: black and white photographs tacked up on a wall.
      The first one is a subway car covered with graffiti, the second
a train platform, deserted, the third a baby owl beneath a sewer grate,
      the fourth a white amaryllis opening before a black door,
the fifth a boy slumped against a chain-link fence, dropping
      the used needle on the ground, the sixth a girl's face

crossed out with an X in red magic marker, the seventh a computer
    screen glowing in an empty room.

When will the hands come to lift her?
    Jailed in the tense vocabulary of capture
she waits for the gentleness to find her and confuse her,
    waits for her hooded journey
                    to resume.

~~~

I have a sack I must not look inside it.

It is of a certain weight and I must carry it with me always.

If I need to wash my hands I must make for the sack a bed a gentle place.

It's harsh what is inside but am I harsh?

When I walk I see the seagrass bending, spineless, willow-thin,

outside of grammar, watery and wind-struck,

outside of any grip.

The weight of the sack instructs me. There are places I can go and places I
                                                  can't go.

I'm heavy and light all at once.

Each day the sun over water sets a little farther to the left

but the weight of the sack doesn't alter.

I carry it but mustn't look inside it.

~~~

A wedding by the sea. The bride dancing on the sand
      in her white dress. Lanterns, gathered wings, up in the trees.
Then her voice from her bed of weeds: please don't leave me. My arms and legs
      rotted long ago, my torso's gone my sex is gone. The salt-sea ate my bones.
Cold as I am, please don't leave me.

And then her sentences suddenly broke, her voice grew softer:

No on, there is none. The tongue-tied, the blindfolded moon. High stakes
                                             but no
onward. Makeshift allegiances. Blindfolded sea, tongue-tied and pulling. Stars
                                                there
are none moon there is none. Was. Wager and was. That sadness I feel now.
                                                    That was.

I sat down beside her, watched the seaweeds turn to coral
      where, through no will of her own, she had touched them,
then I woke.

~~~

56

In the rearview mirror
    the ocean is a strip of film,
        a girl's luminous arm, unreal and pulsing.
A road of water, a graveyard of bright cars. Stifled chorus of the waves,
    their sound turned softly down.
        Then an hour later there are streets again,

these streets laid out with purposefulness, a grid filled with passing eyes
    that look and do not look.
        Streets that are my garment and my wish. I put on the glittery windows
take them off. Put on the street-names, Cornelia, Elizabeth,
    take them off. Pieces of dream—the white body, drowned, but then it
                                  breathes,
    the khaki-colored room—I carry them with me through these streets,
they stick to me I do not put them down.
    A face appears in a window, no one I know, but I carry it with me awhile,
    and the hands hanging laundry from a line
between two buildings, and the girl crying by a trash can,
    her red hands cupped over her whole face

as if with her hands she were trying to make a soft bed for her eyes,

a brief bed of gentleness, bed of leaves and little branches

lifted from the green-blue scrolling sea.

Seaweeds

Before we touched Medusa's head we felt the soft wreckage
of the waves on our bodies, rode with the foam netting and un-netting
us, the stiff trees so strange in their separateness, as if grafted
to a fear we couldn't see. Above us,

stars like passwords, access codes glittering in zones of the unhidden.

Above us: clouds scattering in horrorless dissonance, sun untouched by
footsteps.

We didn't know what it meant to be so savagely self-sealed.

This is the relentless dream, this the admission ticket that can't be given back.
As there are cardinal points that can't be changed, machines that are
programmed
to do just one thing, and one thing only, as there are xeroxes of other xeroxes,
lighter or darker but basically the same,
as there are screens unaltered by the wishes that move through them,
and scenes that can't rescind their harsh configurations,

so, too, we remember from within our rigidity now:

rush

of waves   mapless gatherings of leaves.

We think: That midnight was. The brights between. Plummeting sunshine,
blue amaze.

The waves move through each other without hurting each other.
The sand unbinds itself slowly. Sea roses open.
The minutes impart their vertigo
as summations are given, retracted, then given again.
A child dreams she's swimming through a wall, and the wall is white water.
Eyes move back and forth beneath closed lids.

We think: cloisters of envy   threshold   winding stair.

Escape Velocity

What speed does the spacecraft need to reach its escape velocity,
    breaking completely free
of the ghost-gravity, until it's glassy and dazzling above us,
    becoming that dream-flare we can't reach? Down here
I mark with my markless eyes this earth,

thick shadow of the leafless maple
    on light snow
next to the barely-landmark of the skinny month-old ash.
    They are specificity's remembering, disremembering call.
And here's sunlight on the neighbor's wall, how it's gusting
    fate-like over it,

no feeling within it at all, as it, unsafely, moves.
    Deathmask!—I saw you in a book
freed of any wanting, not thinking of escape or plunder.
    Smooth rounded eyes
tantalized by stillness. Undazzled. Unalarmed. From somewhere

behind me a radio played, the news was updated.
    If I held you and rubbed you would you slowly come apart,
breaking up like static, particle by particle,
    your white dust on the very tip of my insistent finger,
your eyes fading back into the air, taken

wholly back? The absences stalking your
    each dissolving feature,
(mere presence like an abscess breaking)
    while the radio keeps on feeding the air
to fill it with our human life. . . .

But I haven't touched you. I watch from my room the children
    heading home from school, some dragging their bookbags,
others rushing over sidewalks
    as if they might, by some miracle,
suddenly take flight. . . .

But everywhere I look are walls,
    gray walls, and white, and black, and tan
with cracks in them, or bearing the brown residue of
    creeping vines; subtraction's
intricate, digressive tracings. . . .

Last night I walked out onto the porch
    and instead of looking at the sky
watched the houselights on the mountain, how they flickered
    as if trying to gain strength,

nestled, as they were, in green-black forest.
    And I felt for that moment my human place on this earth,
as if those lights and the cold ground
    between them were a bridge that I could walk on,
a crossing neither beautiful nor rapid,

but redolent with a strange joy and love and damage.

Dark Lullaby

In the distance the red blinking light is the radio tower in Randolph
    and below it on the hills   are sparse patches of old farms
pale clearings in the darker greens
    lullaby of order   among the fiercer blackish-greens
and beneath that, white fog, cold dreaming girl who will not wake
    (you must not speak to her, you must not make her wake) her white
dress the cloth of separateness, of sleep

while in the house behind me
    there are so many clicks and whirrs
here in the Information Age
    an e-mail coming in from China now
where someone sits at this very moment
    typing numbered pages into a machine
wrapping us in consequence   though it's evening there
       and we are half the world away.

~~~

The sun as if unhinged from night's suppressive element
    pulses over the eastern pasture
where three horses untethered from anything but day
    rub their heads against each other's necks
to wipe away the swarming flies   while sparrows line up like selling points
    on the phone wires
cutting narrow shadows in the dirt   thin lines much like the demarcations
    of a map's sovereign borders: this is mine it isn't yours
the wind sifting through the horses' manes and raising the hair on my arms
    like a vocabulary moving through a mind to make a landscape

to find where consequence announces itself suddenly, without forethought,
> then moves on.

~~~

In a room overlooking the fields
> one summer I drifted on my bed   and only listened
wind in the maples, in the pines,   suppressive and anxious so it seemed
> though I knew it could feel nothing
but it was also the quotidian kingdom of changefulness   not fearful
> ambivalent lullaby   makeshift song
I was unable to leave my room   every movement frightened me
> Immobilism leaned down   tall in her black dress
her long body an arc before the window   she stroked
> my sweaty hair   as for centuries she had visited countless others
no different from myself   not singing only stroking
> I could hear the barn swallows clattering outside
racket of wings in and out of the barn's roof
> their flight neither trespass nor ambush
and the wind which needs no access code
> which isn't programmed nor heading for a target   always I listened for it
I preferred my sense of hearing   as if my sight were a misprision of
> sight   there were hushes, clicks   sounds pushed each other forward
someone left a tray of food by the door   knocked
> and went away.

~~~

This thrall of light, delirious forager
        at once suppliant and sovereign—

When Maia was two she wanted out of her crib wanted to grab in fistfuls
        morning's light
pounded with her fists, cried, pushed and pushed against the wooden slats.

I laid a mattress on the floor   the light so clean through the window
        as if scoured,
her crib, a broken ribcage, dismantled in the corner.

She woke the next morning to sun, for the first time no boundary
        between her and the light that spread like water on the floor
though where it caught in the wind-flung curtain it seemed heckling and fierce
        like investors that won't let go.

I could hear her laughter, her singing to herself.

~~~

Night. The stars like microchips. The moon so solid, without vertigo, rising above
        the blinking Randolph light.

~~~

"It was always said that the stars were fastened to a crystal vault so they couldn't
fall. Now we have taken heart and let them float on air, without support, and they
are embarked on a great voyage."

64

They look like an instrument panel, blinking. As if there were a destination.
    But I feel the wind on my skin
not as the marking of a stopping place
        but as movement and the commemoration of movement
elegy   offering   dark wish
            the distances swarming with promise   joyful fear.

And Brecht imagined Galileo saying, caught in the thrill and fright of what
        he'd found,

"The universe lost its center overnight, and in the morning it had a countless
number of centers. Now each one can be regarded as a center and yet none can.
For there is a lot of room suddenly."

And in the morning suddenly a lot of room. Overnight and in the morning count-
less. The universe lost, a center yet none. Regarded rooms. Morning, night,
countless and yet none. A countless number then suddenly. The center lost.
Each one regarded yet none is. A lot of centers, each one a morning lost. Lost
numbers overnight and in the morning. Sudden countless room.

I feel the *now* against my skin, its windy contingencies opening   still dreaming
        like the cold girl who covets the white incisions of her dreams
the sun burns her away   but she comes back
        sometimes in pieces   sometimes whole
the white windy cloth of her leaving   billowing somewhere even now
        frame after frame of her
brought up on some screen   to be scrutinized and analyzed
        what is the chemical composition?   what is the ratio of water to light?
(do not speak to her she must not wake she does not want to)
        her silence like the silence of the courtroom long after the gavel's come down

no one on the witness stand   the entire room emptied
        the rows of wooden benches   staring.

~~~

Zone of access codes. Zone of crisis management and weapons inspections.
Zone of conjuring, of faster-than-light and sound waves through water. Zone of
vertigo, of wish. Zone of fluorescence. Zone of stars. Zone of radio frequencies,
of thick pharmaceutical air. Zone of tenderness, of grief. Zone of tax forms.
Zone of maladies, of ghosts. Zone of the sea breaking on a screen, its gravelly
hush an exaggerated breathing, its waves morphing into other waves, the
boundary between here and there dissolving.

~~~

Soft spies of light, soft infiltrators over the hillside's fading green.
        Evening. An ant walks across the wooden deck, pushing a bread crumb
clambering over it   trying another angle   then pushing it again
        its body shiny black as my watchband
or the casing of the rearview mirror
        I watch it awhile   the light lessening as when a hand moves away
from a mouth. . . .
        Is this what candor is   this insect pushing, struggling with its crumb
so small against the accumulations of gigantic leaning things
        and a woman sitting, watching   wondering where it's headed
and will it get there at all   then standing up and walking back into the house
        to make dinner   or to answer the phone.

The Crossing

Now the ghost-bodies are crossing and re-crossing the screen,
    unmoored from this lullaby called solid world,
called touch,
    having capsized into tremor and wish,
meandering through words and words and words
    unspooling as the channels
click.

I like to watch them move,
    part winged, and then part ruptured, so they seem,
their magic kisses putting to sleep the rigid, gilded
    frames. Cloud-chambers, remnants
of wind. There is such wandering, such trespass
    in the light, intentionless or searching.
Scaffoldings, wilderness,
    bright

grief, *the edges of objects flee*, finding no stopping place
    to rest at, no final close-up
ruthless or soothing in its closure,
    only this ongoingness, this fraying further and further
into less than can be seen,
    this incendiary mismanagement
through which the days revise and re-define themselves,
    slipping

past their captions. The bodies on the screen:
    it's as if they want to slip past the background music,
dispersing even further, past the glittery searchlights
    of their time-slots, past the convulsive hiss

that shimmers in the glass, into an air that we can't see,
      an air that glides and purrs with freedom.
The dispersion lures them, whispering *come follow*, and their atoms dance
      to its desire, its critique of being held.

It's so rivery, the world. For a long time I couldn't feel it,
      watching from my fierce concealment.
Then my freeze-framed skin grew slowly restless, and I moved
      at first like the figures on the screen, back and forth, back and forth,
as if a channel could click me
      into place at any moment even as I slipped
away. And then, as I moved differently and more,
      I saw that hope

is astonishment awake, and I heard the dispersion
      whispering to come closer,
and I heard also its soft sisters, how they are always with us,
      their restless scannings, their boundaryless
enchantment, so wild and attendant, so alert.

Tracks

Someone's been getting at these subway cars unwatched
    so that by morning when
they're taken from the train yard
    they're covered with bright defiant
colors that travel through the tunnels
    then up onto the el.
Always I can feel a suppression
    inside myself (*white grove, black grove of ash, white ash*)
that whispery place where the slaughterous reds
    are muffled, starved,

as they drown in the gray air,
    cut off from quickening light or any fire.
But here the subway cars flash their giant
    signatures, decisions: *Partners in Crime* in looping lime-green
letters above the grimy mechanisms
    of the wheels. "You just don't know how badly I want to reach
my hands on a can of spray
    and touch my big train set in my yard
and feel the voltage running

through it while I paint my name
    onto that screen." A reeling hawk, red trees,
and sharp black skyline. Yellow lightning
    sizzling on the closed
pneumatic doors. *Catch me if you can*
    signed Spin and T-Kid, Sonic Bad.
A dollar sign. A gun. *Hand of Doom*, by Seen.
    How they surge by, the pictures,

broken, broken, in the stinging
    ice-white light.

Quiet suppression that seethes in me,
    what does your grove hide,
what does its cottony air, all twilight, all enclosure,
    hide? So quieted that place,
so full of storm-fear, dim mirages,
    while inside you a girl runs wildly toward those tracks
(they are so hidden in your mist she barely finds them)
    and then lies down so close that when the sparks fly
they catch and glitter in her tangled hair.

Walls

As if these walls heard a river and wanted to go to it, become it,
    an urgent self-releasing river, roiling, spilling over—
wanting for themselves such tempests, sweetest stirrings,
    such strayings through an aggregate, bright world.

The walls are so tired of their mission to protect, to safeguard, to keep out.
    What if we were a hummingbird, they think, or small instances of light,
vapors, swirling leaves? What if we could cross-cut through the air,
    could trace the thickets of raspings, and feel how in the headwinds
circling like magics
    we are made and then unmade?

~~~

In the Quinta del Sordo, near the river Manzanares,
    Goya covered his walls
with darkness's elegy to light,
    room upon room of monstrous, reeling
thought. Leering figures in enormous wind-swept robes
    whirl in smoky air
as the fates fly coarsely blurred
    above the earth; one holds a tiny effigy, one a pair
of scissors, one a lens.
    Saturn devours the head of his child.

But radiography shows that covered by these scenes
    brought forth by the mind's intensest beatings, its perilous
stark leaps from cliff to cliff,
    are others he'd first painted, pastoral and calm.

Hidden by the darks are broad green fields, blue skies,
    vast spaces not yet cancelled
by despair. A man with upraised arms lifts his foot to start
    a solitary dance. A smiling woman leafs intently
with bent fingers through a book.

Only then did he paint over them.

~~~

Site of vanishings and dawnings

Of the tree in bloom and its silences in bloom

Of headwinds, fires, rains

Site of rising wings and falling wings

Site of the body swirling barefoot dances through wet grass

Body that sings and weeps as it goes

And mind that thinks nightfall but not mindfall

Yet feels always its own falling

Through brightnesses and darks

And knows that falling, too, to be a dance

~~~

One night I heard her crying in her bed, found her with her knees
    pressed hard against the wall
as if it were a wing that would beat into her
    and which she had, inside her sleep, to push backward
from her heart. Was she awake? It seemed her child-sleep
    was still half-there, half-holding her, half-scattered-off by fright.
Her eyes still closed, she moved her lips, her forehead
    hot and sweaty to my touch, "A beggar kissed me on the head. I was afraid."
But before I could answer, she was once again asleep.

~~~

When the man could no longer walk, when the walls around him
seemed the only witness to his pained and wasted body,
when the chairs ignited at his touch, his flaming touch,

he stared at the blank sheet and wrote, "I am a xerox of my former self. I am no
longer animal, vegetable, or mineral. I am no longer coded and deciphered, no
longer made of circuits and disks. See the signs I try to make with my fingers and
hands. See the vague movements of my lips among the sheets. I can't speak your
language any longer."

Site of vanishings and dawnings

Of the tree in bloom and its silences in bloom

73

Of wings that rise but then they cannot rise

Body that sings and weeps as it goes

Faint shadow that dances, singing and weeping as it goes

~~~

"The sleep of reason produces monsters."

In Goya's etching the man rests his head on his worktable,
    while the walls swarm with his dreams: bats
and weird self-portraits,
    some smiling, others howling
or wincing. And as the dreamer neither chooses nor mischooses
    his dream, he can lean his head so softly on the table,
like one who's merely watchful, surrounded by such beating, restless wings.

~~~

A beggar kissed me on the head. I was afraid. He was leaning against
    a house called the Black House, though it was also called the House
of Beating Wings. He balanced lightly on his crutches that were almost like two
                                                                    sisters,
    two mute and faceless dolls
he'd turned to for some comfort, their heads in lightest
    rest against his chest. His left leg was just a stump

wrapped in dirty bandages, almost like a third, sad sister,
    and I placed into his hand my coin
and then he leaned down to me
    and kissed me.

I felt like I was disappearing, that the wall behind him was a wind that wanted me,
    though I knew I was completely unimportant, nothing that anything should
                                                                        want.

His mouth had sores on it, and some were bleeding. I felt a kindness in his skin
    that was like walls breaking apart, crumbling into chalk, the chalk-bits
                                                                    swirling,

and inside them was a mixture of laughter and of sobs.

~~~

I am no longer coded and deciphered
I hear the tempests, sweetest stirrings
The beggar comes to me and whispers in my ear but I can't understand what he
                                                                    is saying
I feel his lips against my skin
These walls are dark; they see the vague movements of my hands against the
                                                                    sheets
The beggar has three sisters: his crutches and one stump
If I am afraid of him how can I care for him, take care of him?
His lips on my forehead a language I can't speak

I see walls that want to be a river
As once I was a girl who wanted most to be a wall and to feel nothing
When the deaf man painted his walls the birds were singing
What is the sound of blackness stirring?
What do the crutch-girls hear as they're propped against the wall
Their brother dreaming, sleeping?

~~~

Young orchards: apples, peaches, pears.
    Cloud banks scattering
according to their nature; in accordance with the wind, its nature.
    Unsplintered blossomings. Evening Grosbeak. Red-winged Blackbird. Jay.

Body of echoings, unfoldings.

We say nightfall but not mindfall, and yet I feel inside me
    the mindfall hovering, descending,

like walls breaking apart, their hazes, their black winds and moon-brights
                                  glinting

(the small trees slowly fading, disappearing)

in which I hear, "A beggar kissed me on the head. I was afraid."

In which I see his stump, his lips, their chapped and broken stirrings
like small wings, their odd, particulate loveliness.

In which I hear the laughter from the road, the small-talk floating by on airy
                                                                            waves.
In which I hear how in the headwinds, fires, rains,

we are made and then remade, unmade.

Summer Storm

And stay with us for this late-breaking story, said the voice,
      but I was listening to the laughter
of the storm, alchemical and soaring,
      rough afterthought unraveling the flat sunlight.
I was listening to its merciless exposure,
      that moving body reiterating itself over the hills,
the riddles in it, joyful and giddy, so it seemed,
      as it cut and then healed itself
again and again as was its nature. That storm
      that would soon sentence itself to its own ending.

Its healing was a quiet thing. And inside it the lambs
      ate and slept, or walked, and sometimes ran
from one pasture to another. Each mother and her twins
      in small groups within the larger
moving group, their bells
      spilling into each gap and crevice of the silence.

(I am inside a parenthesis, I thought. I am the watcher, apart,
      though I can feel, like them, this cold wind against my skin.)

All day, all night, the lambs are wandering or purposeful
      up and down the hills, running toward tree-clumps
or away, their bells entering my waking
      or filtering into my sleep, luring and lulling
like a tenderness, the promise of a clear and simple demarcation.

"It is the force of gravity that is beautiful in the sea,"
      —I had read this. But in the storm

and even through its aftermath (still echoing),
   I felt a wild disorder so powerfully stalking
the fields and their barbed wire borders,
   forced on by its own laws that seemed to lead to some further
stranger sense, or law—inarticulate, volatile, unsteady.

And all the while the lambs' bells created an order
   within the ongoing disorder of the storm, and I listened
to both, pulled this way and that, like the smashing
   and re-building and smashing of a fence,
until each one seemed insufficiently true without the other.
   The days are trespass,

and their song is made of Darkness mixed with Light.

Inside the Screen

The faces whiten like tensor lights,
      unbruised, as they rise inside the screen
where static wraps its buzzing nets around
      them, hives of buried whispers,
doubt uncured by dream.
      My finger clicks the remote
and other faces

are there waiting, the mica-light
      backgrounding the forward-pointing bodies,
and the ones who've turned away as if in mourning
      for something I can't know.
The light moves, a faint rumor,
      over my skin. *The eye sees not itself*
but by reflection. . . .

Who is it that can tell me who I am?
      Then a click, and they are freeze-framed, here
and here, the background suddenly rigid
      as if stunned,
their gestures no longer shivering out of their
      limbs, but hoarded, stalled,
poor seasons that can't coax each other

forward. But why have I frozen
      them? That I might locate the gaze that doesn't
flee, the face that doesn't swerve
      into facelessness? Are they afraid? What's left

to distract them now that the changefulness
       has gone? Here is the thinness of her wrist,
and here the swerve of panic in his hand. She's

looking into his face and he into hers
       and they cannot turn away. Is it painful
to not turn away? And then I let them
       move again, the background swaying, offering
such sweet distractions: gardens, windows, driveways,
       open doors, as if they didn't have to be
themselves anymore, but a machinery

of comings and goings, mere indications
       of interest or regret. The static-veils comfort them,
confusing the surfaces, keeping them
       apart. My papery skin's so close to them now
as I place my hand against the glass to touch them
       but they can't, inside their glass, be touched,
their mirrory hands rising as if to meet my hand

(I can feel the static buzzing on my skin)
       their faces swimming in their silvery amnesias,
such soft untrammeled bondage whispery, unbroken,
       like swans of another world who've landed here
in this one, our winds rushing over them,
       our eyes lifting to meet the secret light
inside their eyes.

No Threshold

that there is   no threshold

    wind sweeping
the trees   light-glint on grass   the irises blooming   then not
the daylilies blooming   then not
then frost   then gusts of snow

there is wind
       but there is no threshold
as words lead themselves   toward other words
fumbling   radiant   unsure
    enact a wandering
(where am I now? where have I been?)
there is
       no threshold

only voices   inchoate desires
shocking forth

into these things called days
    and the terrain that can't be held by days
neither underworld   nor overworld
but the merciless astonished intertwining
           of both.

~~~

the voice is a wound

it doesn't want to be healed

it is a river a wind a whirlpool a wave

it is Odysseus's foot meeting the hard rocks of a strange
shore

his skin transformed into an old man's skin then back
again

his body battered by waves above the bodies of the
drowned

his body tied to the mast that the singing not destroy him

his body straining even so pulling toward that sound

it is his hands offering a cup of blood to the dead that they might
speak to him awhile

not cower in the shadows but come to him and speak

~~~

the word: passage:
    a romanic formation of *pasare,* to pass

to be allowed or not stopped by a censor

to go on or to proceed in the course of things

that by which a person or thing passes or may pass;
    a way a road a path a route a channel

a negotiation   an interchange

solace of unstillness
    the leaves turning in the wind
and the mind turning

~~~

nights I sat   leaning into the lamplight
    its curative sweep   its gold circumference

beneath which other minds came to me
                    their voices
                        came to me

"since affliction causes everything to be called into question";
"I am free is a contradiction, for that which is not free in me says 'I' ";
"to make of the first reading a blind man's stick. the true reading is the
second one."

she had written this   when the headaches raged in her
when she could find no door to walk through

only days in the fields   among vines
nervous fingers harvesting grapes until nightfall

vines not a door then thickets and sky   not a door

and read through the night other voices not hers
the cat curled beside me
        read of the Bee Maidens   those prophetesses
who would grow angry and tell lies when hungry
        and of the land   at Clairvaux

where "the orchard ends and the garden begins, marked out into rectangles,
or, more accurately, divided up by a network of streamlets;
for although the water appears asleep it is slowly slipping
away." William of Thierry visited there
        who longed to see the face

of his god
        but saw instead "a plague of flies erupt in front of my eyes. . . .
while Your face is ever bent on me in purposeful goodwill
I in my wretchedness am always looking down, so blind withal and lapped in
darkness I do not know how to reach Your presence."

~~~

no doorway   no portal   no key

yet someone's planted rows here

kale potatoes basil leeks

against a backdrop of thickets   a steep hill
        thorns
and hidden
        blossomings throughout

mountains blackening at nightfall   uninhabited even now
though the earth
        thickens with our presence
and the words we have brought to it: tax bracket debt ceiling
the nightmare and dream   of enclosure

the coveting of boundaries

but the wind moves through the branches
                        shelterless   unstill.

Heath

. . . So that it seems there is a heath in me
     where wings and swiftest winds break free above the sparse untended trees,
and the bruise-colored cliffs
     are sorrows that won't speak, though they're unhidden,
where now the scrubby brush grows sticky with pursuing light
     and now a lizard lifts its sturdy head
(does it have offspring? why do lizards seem to move just singly over ground?)
     and now the hint of rain that's not yet come, tender then concussive,
shuddering its hoofbeats, beating wings. . . .

If ground could dream, this ground does harshly dream. . . . The soil glittering
                                                its razor-
     grass, its crevices of darks, its minerals mixing with leaf-mold and spoiled
                                                     flesh,
and a man walking over it, his eyes blinded, his hand held by his daughter,

who's leading him to no place they can find.

If night could wander into day—curious, unbidden, lost—it would touch me
                                                 with its skin,
     much like this man who cleaves now to his daughter
as they walk and walk this glinting, untamed ground.

~~~

And I would be a net,
I would be mesh, a woven thing with holes in it, the caught mixed with the free,
so much escaping, as it must—
though silt still clings,
and salts and butterflies and fish-scales, ash and ash, from places I can't trace,

a net that catches so little of what's there,
sunrise slipping through, and spores, and stars,

so little prisoned by my thought, my meager sight,
or this skin that feels so wavery

like the wind that shudders its high-stakes wager
through the trees. . . .

~~~

Then Antigone said to Oedipus (there on the heath,
rags hanging from his body,
the gentleness and horror and defeat nesting in his wind-burned eyes)

Here, Father, take my hand,
now that we are like this unprotected heath,
or boats the waves continually break over,

we who are blessed and cursed, just and unjust all at once,
our hands so much like beggars

taking and bestowing, both,
the need finally undisguised in us, now that there's nothing left to hide.

Here, Father, take my hand,
the heath is in us, and we'll walk these desolate grasses,
and we will be a net for the wind which batters, tangles, and moves on. . . .

~~~

Where are they going, those cars outside my window, their sound so windy,
   whooshing down the rain-slick road?

Their sound against my skin
   like the breaking of a radiance

sometimes I still dream of whole.
   Their sound like misplaced wings (so very low),

or the faintest reminder of missiles deployed beyond retrieval.
   Their slurring sound that enters me, the brokenness inside it, though the
                                                            sun-fall

gleams unruined through the pane, unfettered as it sweetly goes,
   as once it must have set above that girl

holding her blind father by the hand,
   the ground grown strange beneath their footsteps

as if it had turned restless, so much brokenness inside it, and such stirrings,
   so many rupturings and codes set loose across the ragged, windblown
                                                            slopes.

In the South Bronx

Afternoons I walked past broken signs and bright graffiti,
dayglo signatures scrawled across abandoned buildings,
to the store I worked in—my father's store—
where my tasks were simple because I was a child:
dusting, sweeping, arranging greeting cards on narrow silver shelving.

But what I liked was sneaking off into the stockroom, its secret
dampnesses and darkness, where I waited for each complex trespass
that might find me and hint at something different, something beyond
the custody of money; how it would lead me away from those rigid gleaming
aisles with their orderly objects—some useful, some alluring,

and the register up front full of green and silver.
I'd sit among the empty cardboard boxes, each stack of them
like a mild endangered city slightly swaying,
while I thought of the children's hands, small as my own,
made livid in the store's fluorescent lighting,

and the way they'd hold out their palms so I could count for them
the few coins they'd carried so carefully from home:
Is this enough? Is this? Enough for what their mother
had sent them for: a kitchen clock, a ladle.
And often it was not. I wanted

to turn my face away in shame, but stood and swept
and piled the dirt into a dustpan, swept some more, and watched
how the shelves seemed never to grow empty (magic shelves!)
as they filled with *things*, so many things,
from assembly lines and sweat shops I hardly could imagine.

Each night we'd leave that neighborhood, though we'd once lived there,
riding back in our car toward the suburbs, past crowded neon streets,
and then onto the expressway, until finally we'd glide past the river
that balanced bright strings of light on its surface,
as if there were no hidden waste in it, no washed-up shoes, no broken moorings.

At Niaux

Fists and wounds of light, battlements and ranks of light: we
    leave them outside, wander in with flashlights
whose beams flirt and shiver on the walls. Here is the
    clay floor, slippery, soft, and here
the anxious dark I carry within me as I walk.

The ground bulges as if it did not want
    our footsteps. The drawings of animals are almost a mile
in. Each morning my dreams disintegrate, coming unstuck
    from their sleepy frame, the canvas in flame,
or a film's edges melting and curling as it burns,

but these walls dream their animals unceasingly,
    the chargers, the mothering, the injured ones, the gravid,
the gaping nest of each eye fiercely open.
    We walk on and on.
These flowers are like the pleasures of the world,
    but there are no flowers here. The walls loom up,

half flash-lit, half in dark. A *headless man? The garments*
    of Posthumous? This is his hand, his foot mercurial,
his mortal thigh. . . .
    The walls conspire, make up stories. No. They're murder
without plot, betrayal without motive, the aura of crime
    but not the crime, the humming of it like shockwaves
through water.

Who walks ahead of me? And stops, as if by a river
    whose surface holds the stark

reflected autopsy of stars, or his own face
    lying in its watery distortions,
mouth slightly open, as if wanting to speak. . . .

We have come a long way. We put down our flashlights, shut them off
    to conserve battery power, the guide writing in a book
the time of our arrival in this far chamber
    of the cave, her light the only light now,
the black air behind us crawling over itself
    and over itself,

while the animals rise up beneath her beam, streaked and fleshed
    onto the walls, fetlocks, horns, candor of unchained
instances, graceful summations
    in this velvety unyielding hiddenness,
not roughed up by doubt or vertigo.

I remember, *'Twas but a bolt*
    of nothing, shot of nothing . . . the dream's still here.
But this is not a dream. Most delicate and fiercest venturing,
    how did you come to make these animals that don't
fade? Reindeer, bison, and horses moving off
    into the blackout that won't kill them,

the blackout advancing, caressing the wreckage and the leaping,
    whatever is brought to it, anything at all, our hands,
our faces, anything,
    the blackout singing, taking it all in.

"To Telle Him Tydings How the Wind Was Went"

Restless stirrings. Shadows of branches, wing tips, leaves, moving, tired
                                                    explorers,
    over the ground, as if seeking some entranceway,
to find for a while safe harbor, though the surface is always whispering,
    entreating, so filled with possibilities, beginnings,
and also the tender gold light, the tender sweep of one thing
    into another, calmative, adaptive, that love — ringed with silences and the
                                                    hushed
or violent breakages; insatiable, unfettered scrawls. . . .

~~~

Wind, I feel your cold ravenings, wordless, unprognostic. Your skin meaning
neither yes nor no. Meaning onward, but there can be no resolution. Then
                                                    quietness
a moment — where are you? A softness in you, like the fear of being bruised.
And then you are back again. Your burning skin. Your stopless turnings. My skin
burning under you. My skin that wants to be lifted out of its numbness, being
                                                    burned.

~~~

Love is movement.

When Eurydice fell back, she fell back into a smoky stillness.

I imagine no wind there, only one hand touching the other, her right hand

on her left, forever and ever. In her mind a burning cliff she wouldn't touch.

Its redness scorched her, sometimes it crumbled into the sea but always

it came back. Whispering sister, whispering love. Its ash over her skin,

covering, not restive. Its ash, flat as envy untransformed, graying her hair,

whispering alone, you are alone. And still the cliff burned. Like a warning, like
                                                                    a wish.

~~~

The word "I" is a painful word, I think. Scary to think of.
You can almost hear the solitude
hardening like ice inside it, its wintery underpinnings, its vast spaces,
and always inside it the stranger who can't speak; no words are the right words.

The ninth letter of the alphabet. As in imperator, incisor. As in interest,
intransitive, island, independent.
A shock inside it, always burning, because it knows that it must feel and wander,
how it needs to be intent on something, anything at all,

or the vastness starts to grow even vaster, even emptier,

and the wind dies down, the to-and-fro falters and dies down like a beggar slowly
                                                                    weakening,

holding out his empty, crusted cup.

~~~

You must breathe into the machine
and the machine will measure your breath, its weakness or its strength.
I sat in the machine; it was a glass enclosure.
I blew into a tube.
The attendant was wearing a white coat. I heard him through a speaker
inserted in the booth.
My lungs were like a woman who wants to walk onto a heath
but turns away. My lungs were Eurydice's dream
where the world as she's known it has been cast off like an amputated limb—
Why walk onto the earth-crust, its desolate surfaces, from which the world
has been so harshly torn away? Not even the wind is left on it, not even the
                                       sunlight, the rain. .. .

~~~

Wind, you do not click from channel to channel. You are not bound and
                                              gagged.
You're eyeless yet still watchful, figuring it this way, figuring it that. Bright
                                            scalder,
usurper, you prosper and contend. Ladders are too orderly for you. Stairs
                                      and walls
too orderly for you. You disarrange and disarrange. You would take these words
                                        and
scramble them, until I must lose what I know or think I know: channel not
                                      bound or
gagged too orderly the lungs a weakness in the earth-crust desolate surfaces
                                    amputated limb—

~~~

Ghosts and gaps. The eye's so small, so narrowly focused.
The world sends bits of itself plunging in then past it,
bearing its torn posters, limbs, negotiations.

It slips and slides, my eyes two traps
waiting for their smallest prey.

And then I feel I am a ghost who stands and watches,
wavery, unskeletoned, and always sidelined, always incomplete,

as I watch the footprints extending far beyond where I can see,
wind entering their mild declivities,

nesting, calm, then moving gamely on. . . .

~~~

Wind gusted through the unsealed tomb, over the golden combs and mossy
                                                                    statues,

clay pitchers, hairpins, jewels,

and over the wrapped body, its secretive fingertips, its mute, infolded stories.
Unwary ambassador, it grazed the emptied eyes, the spices filling each orifice,
the disavowals, the surcease, the lost name.

~~~

So still this night. So like a blindness.

What can I belong to? What can I be the commodity of? Where is the price tag
I can wear?

Will I feel safe then, will I, if I wear it?

And then the wind picks up, scrambling all I know, reminding me of all I do not
know,

the stories breaking, the stories battered, until, from inside them,

a small voice begins to speak. . . .

The Subway Platform

And then the gray concrete of the subway platform, that shore
    stripped of all premise of softness
or repose. I stood there, beneath the city's sequential grids
    and frameworks, its wrappings and unwrappings
like a robe sewn with birds that flew into seasons of light,
    a robe of gold
and then a robe of ash.

All around me were briefcases, cell phones, baseball caps,
    folded umbrellas forlorn and still glistening
with rain. Who owned them? Each face possessed a hiddenness.
    DO NOT STEP ACROSS THE YELLOW LINE; the Transit Authority
had painted this onto the platform's edge
    beyond which the rails

gleamed, treacherous, almost maniacal,
    yet somehow full of promise. Glittery, icy, undead.
Sharp as acid eating through a mask. I counted forward
    in my mind to the third rail, bristling with current
hissing inside it like a promise or a wish; and the word
    forward as if inside it also,

as if there were always a forward, always somewhere else
    to go: station stops, exits, stairways opening out into the dusty
light; turnstiles and signs indicating this street
    or that. Appointments. Addresses. Numbers and letters
of apartments, and their floors. Where was it, that thing I'd felt
    inside me, tensed for flight
or capture, streaked with the notion of distance and desire?
    And the people all around me, how many hadn't

at some time or another curled up in their beds with the shades drawn,
    not knowing how to feel the forwardness, or any trace
of joy? Wing of sorrow, wing of grief,
    I could feel it brushing my cheek, gray bird
I lived with, always it was so quiet on its tether.
    Then the train was finally coming, its earthquaky
rumblings building through the tunnel, its focused light

like a small fury. Soon we would get on, would step into
    that body whose headlights obliterate the tunnel's dark
like chalk scrawling words onto a blackboard.
    I looked down at the hems of the many dresses all around me,
they were so bright! Why hadn't I noticed them before? Reds
    and oranges and blues, geometrical and floral patterns

swirling beneath the browns and grays of raincoats,
    so numerous, so soft: *threshold*, I thought, and *lullaby, disclosure,*
the train growing louder, the feet moving toward the yellow
    line, the hems billowing as the train pulled up,
how they swayed and furrowed and leapt
    as if a seamstress had loosed them like laughter from her hands—

A NOTE ABOUT THE AUTHOR

Laurie Sheck is the author of three previous books of poetry, the
most recent of which, *The Willow Grove,* was a finalist for the
Pulitzer Prize. Her work appears widely in such journals and
magazines as *The New Yorker, The Kenyon Review* and *Boston
Review.* The recipient of fellowships from the Guggenheim
Foundation, the National Endowment for the Arts and the Ingram
Merrill Foundation, among other institutions, Sheck has been a
member of the creative writing faculty at Princeton University
and currently teaches in the M.F.A. program at the New School.
She lives in New York City.

A NOTE ON THE TYPE

The text of this book was set in Electra, a typeface designed by
W. A. Dwiggins (1880–1956). This face cannot be classified as
either modern or old style. It is not based on any historical model;
nor does it echo any particular period or style. It avoids the
extreme contrasts between thick and thin elements that mark
most modern faces, and it attempts to give a feeling of fluidity,
power and speed.

Composed by Creative Graphics, Allentown, Pennsylvania
Printed and bound by Edwards Brothers, Ann Arbor, Michigan
Designed by Virginia Tan